Connor Miller and Cheyenne Barton

SUSTAINABLE LOOPS:
Getting It Together Without Falling Apart

Sustainable Loops:

Getting It Together Without Falling Apart

———————

written by Connor Miller

designed & illustrated by Cheyenne Barton

CONTENTS

~~~~

AN INTRODUCTION

Most days, I wake up with a question in my brain and I go out into the world and find answers to that question. Most recently, I've been thinking, "Why am I working a 9-5 job?" There are seemingly endless avenues for work that can be done from anywhere, at any time. I look online and see a handful of folks running their own businesses and making a living in ways that were not possible ten years ago. So, I went out and asked these people how they did it.

Many of these folks were young and creative, and a lot of them struggled with being their own boss. There is no handbook for the kind of work that they're attempting to do solo, so some things are very difficult for them to accomplish. But, every once in a while, I'll happen upon a young entrepreneur who has figured out an aspect of their online business that really works, and it's these tools that I'm hoping to bring together and share in this book.

Not a lot of the people I interviewed had it "figured out" (especially the ones who seemed to be the most successful). Even with great sales, reach, and products, I found that many creative movers/shakers had trouble finding balance in their lives. They were, after all, attempting to run a fully fledged venture on their own.

I haven't really figured it all out either. But this book is a journalistic exploration into experiments and tools that work for me and my friends. I hope that getting all of this information in one place at the very least helps navigate some of the more common problems I've heard about, and together we can work towards shaping our careers in innovative and flexible ways.

About me

I'm a writer, organizer, and collaborator. Originally from the San Francisco Bay Area, I went to college in New York and dropped out after two-and-a-half years. Unsure of what to do next, I moved to the Pacific Northwest where I haunt cafes, work odd jobs, and write.

In this time, I published three books, launched several startups, and did journalistic research into business, investment firms, and entrepreneurship. I interviewed everyone I could and blogged about what I found out, giving me a cursory sense of the business terrain among my peers.

Again, my qualifications to speak on any of the topics in this books are from in-the-field research paired with an exhaustive amount of reading. I'm looking to create a toolbox, not a recipe for success. And hopefully, through all my digging, I can share with you what I found here, in *Sustainable Loops*.

SUSTAINABLE LOOPS

A lot of what you read in this book will hinge on the concept of creating "sustainable loops". This is not a spin-off of Froot Loops (delicious as they may be), but instead the concept of getting into a life rhythm that can be repeated indefinitely. Too many of my friends (and myself) have been subject to burnout. We work too hard, spread ourselves too thin, and then up having destructive breakdowns that are not good for anyone. An example: I dropped out of college. It was my third year at school and I worked so hard every night, partied too hard on weekends, and at the end of the day I really couldn't pay for the education I was getting. The winter of 2013, I cried outside of the administrative office in the snow, on the phone with my sister asking "What am I supposed to do? I can't do this anymore." Long story short, the way I was working was not sustainable.

Nowadays, I have a job with a predictable work schedule. I carefully track how much money I make against how much money I spend. I sleep a lot. I rest a lot. I make sure I buy little gifts for myself and do things that make me happy for happiness's sake. The emphasis is finding a rhythm, a repetitive loop that makes me feel fulfilled. Done are the days in which I feel strung out, hopeless, and unsure of what's going to happen the next day. Sustainable. Fucking. Loops.

With your lifestyle (or even your business if you have one) you should always be asking yourself, "Is this sustainable?" If you are a creative, a freelancer, or someone who works for themselves, YOU are your most valuable resource. Your business depends on your ability to wake up in the morning and to execute the core functions of your business. This means you MUST take care of yourself. Which means checking in emotionally. Which means being kind to yourself. Which means realizing that sometimes you need to stop working and just bingewatch BoJack Horseman.

Re: SUSTAINABLE LOOPS

WHAT ARE my LOOPS?	
WHERE ARE my AREAS OF BURNOUT?	
WHAT IS NOT SUSTAINABLE?	
WHAT WOULD a SUSTAINABLE LOOP LOOK LIKE?	

goals

Goals are and one of the most difficult things to manage. We are often afraid to make decisions or to focus energy towards just one goal. Committing time and effort to project can be daunting, especially when it isn't clear whether or not it will all work out in the end. If you are like me, you want to do one hundred things all the time. So, start by writing them down.

> my goals:

When you get the space to, write down all of them. Big and small, you should ALWAYS make lists of the things you want to do.

Writing down your goals helps you orient yourself. Once we get rolling with our experiments, you will constantly have to refocus and redefine your goals. Your goals can be as vague as "figure out what I like", or they can be as specific as "fix my bed every morning." The key is to write them all down. This makes them more real and allows you to reference them for your own personal accountability. If you ever feel overwhelmed with possibility, making lists and writing everything down helps make the ethereal slog of your creative brain into something manageable. It goes onto paper, where it can rest easy and you don't have to worry about it any more. I'll write my list here for you to look out to get an idea of how this works.

example 1. CONNOR'S GOALS

WEEKLY GOALS
 * check out that new café
 * make lunches every day this week
 * make coffee at home during the week
 * blog at least once

MONTHLY GOALS
 * get a rough draft of my novel done
 * minimize expenditure on dining out
 * get a new pair of glasses

LONG-TERM GOALS
 * start investing
 * get a good year-round wardrobe
 * find a more permanent home

Values

I'm going to encourage you to make choices, and choices mean that you will have to reflect on what you really value. For example, if you are going to choose between getting coffee every day at your favorite cafe vs. buying a really nice pair of shoes, you will have to hold these two things on balance and determine which one you value more.

My values have changed a lot over the years. For a while I valued creativity, then career, then "authenticity" whatever that means. I tried to make choices based on my values which I re-examined and tweaked as I moved forward in my life.

Now, I value stability. This means putting away a percentage of my money away towards savings, so that when something unexpected and shitty happens, I don't go crazy trying to figure out how to manage the chaos. I value my community, so I spend time and money on things like my blog and on going to certain cafes where I can engage with like-minded folks.

I value coffee, I value my relationships, and I value all the time I spend on my creative pursuits. This helps bring into focus how I spend my finite resources. It's all about what you value. So, what do you value? You don't have to think too hard on this, but try and identify the things that you enjoy and like spending your time and money on. What are the things you hope to see more of in the world? What products do you like to consume? What kind of things do you like to produce? It's a broad question, but less broad than waking up and attacking each day with a machete, not knowing why you're doing what you are doing or where you're going.

WHAT ARE YOUR VALUES?

- _____
- _____
- _____
- _____
- _____
- _____
- _____
- _____
- _____
- _____

Time management

This is huge. Time management will change your life. Many busy, creative people will tell you that the one thing they wish they had more of was TIME. Time is a finite resource, and so much of our personal achievements depend on how we spend our time. While money is a resource, time is something that we can harness to build upon our financial spending power. To spend your time in a smart way is almost the same as spending money in a smart way. The goal is to spend your time/money on things that you value, or things that can potentially bring in greater returns.

One of my least favorite teachers in high school used to pound his fists on his desk and yell out "TIME MANAGEMENT! This will be the key to success in college and throughout your life!" As much as I hate to admit it, Teacher X was right. So much of my success is dependent on how I spend my time. So, now that you've already charted out your goals and your values, it's time to figure out how to divide up your time to make your moments fulfilling and purposeful.

Getting started & motivated

As a creative person, you probably have a Big Idea. This Big Idea is valuable because of the vastness of its scope, and you likely wish you could put this idea into action today. You can. And you will. Will you finish implementing the Big Idea today? No. And realizing this is the key to getting started.

Paralysis and doubt all flood in when we try to accomplish the Big Idea in a day. It will feel impossible and we will get discouraged and the project will dissipate into dust. Start small and begin by doing one thing. If every day you do a Small Thing, you will one day wake up with a more complete Big Idea.

I just met up with a talented creative human being named Brittany. Brittany does it all—music, film, project management. She wants to get her creative career moving with a documentary she's working on. She even already has made some headway on the project! She has hours and hours of film saved, enough for a 30-minute segment or even a feature length film. But while balancing her other projects and her day job, she doesn't know if she has time to commit to the Big Idea.

When talking to her, I suggested that she start with the **Smallest Possible Step** (which we will discuss more later). Why not put together a 2min 30sec trailer for the documentary? This way she has a shareable nugget of media to show to others in case they want to help her with the full-length documentary. This is a way more achievable step, which in turn makes the act of getting started that much easier.

Getting started is hard, but sustaining momentum is harder. If you want to embark on a project correctly, one of the best things you can do for yourself is to work in small, repeatable steps. Do this every day and one day you will be surprised to find yourself at your destination.

The Big P: Procrastination

I don't procrastinate. It's a point of interest for a lot of my friends, because they find it funny. Some people believe procrastination is unavoidable. It's not. I feel ridiculous talking about it because I have reached a point in my life that if I am assigned a task, I do the task in a timely fashion. When I sit down to write, I don't fuck around on Facebook for an hour before I start. I sit down, I plant my feet, I don't even pick music, I just do whatever the fuck I'm supposed to do.

I don't want to intimidate you with this, but instead show you that it is possible to sit down and get to work. I am googling procrastination right now just to make sure I fully understand the concept because this whole phenomenon is a little bit foreign to me. The internet is telling me that procrastination is "the act of delaying or postponing something." Just don't do it. We're going to look at some examples and try some experiments to see if we can minimize the amount of time we procrastinate. I have a ton of strategies for how to get around a general reluctance to do things, which I will share below.

The Smallest Possible Step

Let's imagine you have a ten-page writing assignment due in a week. What most people will do is wait two days before the paper is due and then scramble at the last minute to hammer together a piece of garbage that they will turn in and feel shitty about. You are better than this. Don't do this. As we always do, we are going to make a list, which divides the act of writing the paper into the smallest possible steps.

1. Create and name the document.
2. Write the title.
3. Outline the paper.
4. Do one piece of research. Take notes.
5. Do another piece of research. Take notes.
6. Do a third piece of research. Take notes.
7. Review the outline and make sure we're good to go in writing the paper.
8. Write a rough draft of the paper.
9. Rest.
10. Edit the paper.
11. Rewrite the paper.
12. It's honestly great at this point, but if you have extra time, maybe read one more text and do another re-write.
13. Turn in the paper.

This may look like a lot of work, but in reality it isn't. If you start early and move through small, manageable steps, you will be astounded at how much free time you have, and at your ability to actually produce a piece of work that isn't bullshit. Can you imagine?! Writing something that you are actually proud of and spent time working on? Holy shit! It's like what school should actually be like!

By dividing large tasks into small steps, you gain confidence and momentum with each step you finish. This increases the likelihood that you will complete a seemingly impossible task, because it immediately appears more manageable when divided up into smaller pieces.

I had a mentor who taught me this, and recommended that I use the small-step approach if I wanted to go to the gym more often. The first step was waking up at the time I would ideally go to the gym. The next day I woke up at the right time and put on gym clothes (but I still didn't go to the gym!). The third day's task was waking up, putting on gym clothes, and touching the front door of the gym. It sounds stupid, and it felt stupid, but it was way more manageable and helped me gain confidence to develop a sustainable gym habit, as opposed to trying to go from 0 to 100 in a day. How shitty would it be to wake up one day and just go directly into a gym regimen? Some people do it, but it also increases the likelihood that you will miss a day and feel shitty about it and lose momentum. YOU KNOW THIS IS TRUE. So take small steps.

> BREAK IT DOWN <

PROJECT: _____

SMALLEST POSSIBLE STEPS

1. _____
2. _____
3. _____
4. _____
5. _____

[ILLUSTRATOR'S NOTE: Cheyenne would like to add that she has fallen victim to the shitty-losing-momentum feeling countless times. Slow and steady is always the way.]

Plotting Out Time

We will end up talking a lot about scheduling in this book, but in relation to procrastination, it is important to have designated times to work on tasks. Sometimes we convince ourselves that we don't have time to write our paper. This is bullshit. I am sure you are busy but it is likely that you also spend a lot of your unscheduled moments dithering on the internet. If you have a task, plot out one-to-two hour windows for you to work on said task. Tailor it to be a timeframe that works for you, and put it in your planner or your Google Calendar. Show up and do The Smallest Possible Thing during this time period. Do this for every time block you schedule. These tiny tiny steps add up, and soon you will have a wealth of confidence in your ability to do incredible things. Set aside time and show up. Take small steps.

"How do I work?"

Ideally, yes, you want to wake up at 6:00am, go to the gym, shower, type your best selling novel, eat a healthy breakfast, then go to work. After work you want to make a healthy dinner, unwind, and maybe do some more creative work! Or just relax. Who knows?

Cue record scratch. Is this reasonable? Is this actionable? Is this possible? Is this how you work?

I will never forget an internship I had in New York City. At 3:00pm, EVERY DAY, ON THE DOT, a small bowl of chocolate candies would appear on the break room table. I never saw who put the candies there, but there they were. Every day. Like clockwork.

The rationale was that at around three, most people experience "post-lunch dip", a sensation of fatigue caused by metabolizing one's lunch and also from six hours of being at your day job. The 3:00pm candies was one of the smartest workarounds for post-lunch dip I had ever seen. What if we all could recognize our patterns, the moments when we get distracted or tired and navigate around them?

A friend of mine used to have dramatic breakdowns every Wednesday night. Every. Wednesday. Night. Their parents knew about this and told me that the best way to placate these Wednesday breakdowns was to encourage food and rest. Turns out that Friend X just would worry about all the homework due by Friday and get all worked up about it until it all came to a head on Wednesday night. Realizing that this was a thing helped solve the problem. Seeing the pattern showed that there was a problem in the weekly life design. Friend X was very talented, and finally was able to see that if this happened EVERY WEDNESDAY NIGHT then maybe there were ways to plan for it or to even solve the issue.

We all have our own versions of post-lunch dip or Wednesday Night Breakdowns. And the best way to work around them is to recognize them, honor them, and make small steps towards finding an actionable solution to navigate them.

Know yourself

Many rappers will constantly push an agenda of "know yourself," and I'd really like for you to be on that same level. Below is a worksheet I've provided for you to fill out your day and how you work. Awareness is the first step. Action is the second.

It is SO MUCH easier to make changes or adjustments to your schedule when you know yourself.

When I'm working, I know that there is a point when I hit a wall. I am sitting in front of my computer and the words aren't coming and typing feels like pulling teeth. Sometimes I can muscle through it. But a lot of the time I can't. When I hit my wall, it feels horrible. Everything I write sounds stupid, I scroll through the internet hoping to get inspiration and instead I get distracted. This is no bueno. Something needs to change.

Now that I know that this wall exists, I can implement experiments to get around it. Ideation comes into play here. I can write out a small list of actionable solutions to work around my wall. Heck, now that I know that the wall is here, I can identify it and act accordingly. I'm going to spare you the details and cut to the chase: walking away always helps. Like actually physically walking away. I either go to a new location or walk around the block, and when I sit back down at my computer, I am almost always refreshed. This is a super small and effective solution. Instead of banging my head against a keyboard for two hours, I can take a walk for ten or twenty minutes and come back to slay the game.

One more example: When I get off work, I am impossibly tired. I eat dinner and settle into bed. I'm a very productive person and I want to work at night. But I am also an obsessive person who tends to get involved in things and loses track of time. Because I know myself in this sense, I know that if I work at night I will feel like garbage the next day. So, through knowing myself, I sleep guilt-free and wake up the next morning knowing I will get a ton of obsessive-creative work done.

Some of my creative friends make the "night owl" shift work for them. They swear that some of their most brilliant moments of inspiration have come to them at 2am. Cool. Good for you. That's not how I work. I will show up at 7:00am and I invite my muses to join me. You all can have your 2:00am strokes of brilliance. I need my sleep.

My rule, as a result, is no "work" after 6pm. Sure, I do it sometimes, but I count it as "extra credit" rather than my mandatory productivity period. Any work I do after 6:00pm is bonus, and not essential. This way, I can watch Bojack Horseman guilt-free, and wake up the next morning focused and ready to write. How do you work? I suggest you keep a journal or note in your phone open to highlight the times you have free or when you feel exhausted. Then, with a clear head, map out how you can harness your natural rhythms for maximum creative output. Here's a worksheet for that!

PRODUCTIVITY LOG

example

Time	TASK	NOTES (how i'm feeling)
9:20 am	e-mail	i think it's too early in the day to get caught up in e-mail

Scheduling

I live and die by Google Calendar. Whenever my friendships breach into new levels of intimacy, usually I launch into a bit about how much I love calendars. It's true, it's a little embarrassing, but I definitely think that working in Google Calendars is my superpower. In college, I had a small business in which I would assemble my friends' work calendars for the semester. Sometimes my research in lifestyle design just feels like an excuse to look at calendars. A perfect morning for me is sitting down at my favorite café, popping open my Chromebook, and looking through my weeks and months, imagining the orbits of my life.

You get the idea.

You don't have to plan out *everything* and honestly you probably shouldn't. Life happens in the margins of our plans, and as you will read later, a little bit of spontaneity is good for the soul. But, there are certain things that need to get done. Like laundry. Like grocery shopping. Like going to the DMV. By scheduling all of the boring things you have to do, you free up your availability for all of the other things that "come up".

One of my saving graces is my early morning "business hour". From 7:30am-8:30am every day, I have an open chunk of time to write, send e-mails, journal, or do whatever clerical tasks that need to be done in order for my life to function. Sundays at 3:00pm is my "appointment window" when I schedule most of my coffee meetings or interviews for my blog. Monday is my big "task day" where I go to all the places I need to (the optometrist, the bank, etc). This way I'm never running around with my head cut off over stuff that needs to get done. I have windows for when I can do specific things, and if I don't have anything for those windows, I read or write.

All of my "fun stuff" is typically scheduled after 6:00pm, which is very good for my brain. In this time block, I can get a haircut, watch TV, hang out with friends, whatever, because I have my business hour in the morning and know that any other important tasks will be taken care of on Monday. By creating a skeletal schedule, I have become happier and free.

A little bit each day

If you don't already know who Andy Dufresne (doo-FRAYN) is, here's the short of it: he is a fictional character from the movie The Shawshank Redemption and (SPOILER) he is most famous for his ability to escape prison by whittling away through the wall with a spoon. This fictional story helps demonstrate a lot of how I think we can work. The key is to do a little bit each day. Sometimes it's so little that it feels stupid. But it still feels like something, and it is. All the little things you do each day add up. To further the Andy Dufresne metaphor, we are all in a prison of some sort, but we all can spend a little time each day whittling away at our side projects, or whatever is going to help us get out of whatever entrapments we are currently in.

Writing books is very difficult. I know Jack Kerouac managed to sit down and write On The Road in a single sitting, but most of us don't have access to hard stimulants and that much free time. One of my favorite things to do is participate in National Novel Writing Month (or NaNoWriMo). In the month of November, writers from all over the world set out to write 50,000 works in one month. 50,000 words is the length of a moderate commercial novel, and writing 50,000 words is no small feat. For myself, the only reasonable way to accomplish this is to write roughly

1,700 words a day, which is still a lot, but comparatively little in comparison to writing 50,000 words.

My point is that we (you and me) are big-idea people. We know exactly what we want our project to look like in the end. The hard part is doing all the work that brings us there. I am notoriously impatient so I am constantly looking for shortcuts to get to my destination. With writing books, there are no real shortcuts. You just have to show up every day and write a little bit more. Even if one day it's just a sentence, that's still something.

Conversely, a little bit each day can go against you as well. I am totally misremembering the details of this story, but it's a fairy tale about a man who ignored the fact that a couple grains of sand would fall into his driveway every day, until one day the pile of sand was so big it was nearly impossible to move. Bad habits are like this. If you are doing something small every day that is negatively affecting you, all those grains of sand add up.

So, what's the lesson here? Carefully examine what you do with your days. There are without a doubt a ton of great bestselling books on how to create habits, and I implore you to pick them up or just to actively think about how your daily life adds up to your lifetime. So, we should focus carefully on the structure of our daily, weekly, and monthly schedules to see what we can accomplish in our lives.

Know when to stop

When I am writing, there is a point where I no longer have any more words in me. After a good writing session (which is usually sustained for an hour to an hour-and-a-half), I will find myself scrolling through Facebook or dithering around in my e-mail and basically avoiding writing. This is a sign to me that I probably need a walk, a change of location, or a different project to focus on for the rest of the day. If I power through and write more, sure I'll get more words on the page but I'll hate doing it and the next time I want to write I'll probably remember how shitty it was to force myself to write more than I could at that moment.

One of the best things you can do yourself is take breaks and to notice when you don't have any more creative chutzpah to power you through your next step. SUSTAINABLE LOOPS. Imagine coming to work every day energized because you knew when to stop and you properly recharged your creative engine? You will then develop a positive association with work and probably end up doing more of it in the long run. By not cracking the whip and pushing yourself into overdrive every time you work, you will be happier, more productive, and generate better results.

WHAT aRe some SIGNS I
SHOULD PROBaBLy STOP WORKING?

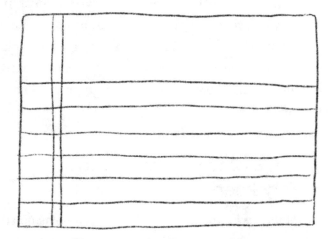

CHAPTER THREE

ORGANIZATION

So, we have already discussed strategies as far as how to organize your time. Now, let's begin to organize our belongings. Things often fall into disarray, and this is sometimes feels unavoidable. The more we clean, the worse we feel when things get dirty again. There are tons of books on how to get organized, most notably *The Life Changing Magic of Tidying Up* by Marie Kondo, which has a specific emphasis on putting everything in its place. I am going to focus on more specific strategies that are less tied to home-making and more tied to getting your professional self together and focused.

The kinds of things you should probably keep

Can I find this info on the internet? Is this information that I can get by making a phone call? These are some questions you can ask yourself when looking through all the paperwork and junk you have on hand. In the same way that Strunk & White beg you to "omit needless words", you should relentlessly throw away things you don't need or use. HOWEVER, our focus will be on keeping the things that are directly useful to your career. This means creative work, documentation on your qualifications, and anything that can be added to some kind of portfolio.

The document tub

One of my pride and joys of my room are my two document tubs. One is marked "Financial" but basically contains any kind of useful clerical documentation for taxes, healthcare, and work. The other tub is marked "Writing", and it contains just that: all of my creative written work. I have manuscripts, attempts at screenplays, old notebooks, you name it. Austin Kleon has a document tub that he calls his "Swipe File", where he keeps bits and scraps of artistic inspiration that he would like to borrow from. The purpose is to have some sort of analog filing system to keep the things worth keeping.

One of the benefits of having these document tubs is simply pride. It feels good to have your shit together in one place, neatly divided by subject or date. It is painful and disheartening to open a box or drawer and see an overwhelming stack of unorganized papers. The simple act of putting things in their place makes me feel more competent and professional, and I suspect it will help you as well. The same way that fixing your bed in the morning sets the tone for your day, having all your documents organized is a huge motivator to do good work.

Digital file management

The key to managing all the files in your computer is to give them meaningful names. I know that file management is kind of silly when you can just type in keywords in a search bar in order to find stuff, but I like thinking about my workspaces like a chef's mise en place. "A messy workstation means a messy brain," says Anthony Bourdain (probably). That being said, your files and folders on your computer should make sense, and you should take time at least once every couple of months to make sure everything follows some sort of organizational flow.

Of of my favorite phrases is "emergent systems" (from Joi Ito & Jeff Howe's *Whiplash*). When you have a bunch of files and are making a bunch of work, patterns emerge. It is silly to make a bunch of folders for files that don't exist yet. The order of things should go as follows: make a mess, make a better mess (Austin Kleon). This way you are also being productive instead of procrastinating by making everything tidy.

The tangible takeaway from this is to just make folders as you need them, then take time once a month to look back and see how everything shakes out. Move some files, rename some folders, and learn how to name your documents in a way that makes it easy to revisit or reference them.

Journals & notebooks

Laptops are formal work environments. Analog notebooks and journals are invitations to play, and **play is perhaps one of the most important parts of creative work**. Even better, it is *way better* to pull out a notebook and write an idea than to open your laptop or make an iPhone note. There are plus sides to each kind of notation, but when you are writing in a notebook you are a) slowing yourself down in order to think clearly b) freeing yourself from the predetermined channels that working in a phone or a laptop tends to lead to and c) you are bringing a tactile experience to writing the information down, making it more tangible.

Because it helps the brain SO MUCH get in the mode of creative thinking, it is a good idea to have a stack of blank notebooks around for easy access. One for your pocket, one for your backpack, maybe even a big one to draw in at home. Sitting at a computer can get you in the habit of limiting your imagination when all you have to work with is a keyboard and a screen. As useful as these tools are, you can come back with more creativity and a refreshed sense of purpose by taking time to doodle in the margins of a notebook.

For example, in writing this book, I had to make a lot of worksheets. I knew what I wanted them to look like, but it would be kind of a pain in the ass to outline them all out in Google Sheets. It was much quicker to just do rough sketches on paper, so that I could come back to my Google Sheets with a clarified design objective.

RUNNING A PROFITABLE SIDE-HUSTLE

This is one of many dreams: to have a business that runs itself and brings in enough money for you to get "fun stuff". Most of the people I talk to work 9-5 jobs but realize that there is potential to have a business-y Instagram and to get money from doing things that you'd often spend time doing anyway. You, as a person who has a smart phone, may have noticed that some people have figured this out already. You may have seen people who make a living from generating content and products which they monetize through available platforms. This is an art form, and one that I still haven't really figured out. But since everyone is trying, I managed to ask around to see what works and also to see what we can do to position ourselves a little bit better in order to make coffee money while we're riding the bus.

34   *Sustainable Loops*

The not-so-secret secret to business

Cheyenne (hi Cheyenne!) runs a successful online business in which she sells stickers and other pieces of art to her Instagram following. She often is often amazed that she is able to do what she does, but her fans love her work and she loves making it and at the end of the day people love spending what they can on the stuff that Cheyenne makes. Aspiring illustrators and other creators reach out to Cheyenne on a regular basis and ask her for advice. How is it possible to do what she does? How can I run a profitable one-person operation through selling art?

"At the end of the day, I make a product that people are willing to pay for. And that's the long and short of it," she tells me. This feels kind of blunt and obvious, but let's examine it. Let's pretend that I write a bunch of poems that I post on Instagram and want to sell small books of poetry containing them. I have 500 followers and get about 23 likes per poem. I want to sell zines to this audience, but the evidence shows that, well, probably only my friends are going to buy the books and I'm not going to make that much money. On the other hand, let's say instead of poems I am uploading one-minute videos of easy vegan recipes. After a month of sharing content, I have 5,000 followers and an average of 300 likes for each post. I'm pulling these metrics out of thin air, but it doesn't take a scientist to see that the likelihood that I can sell a cookbook much easier than a chapbook in this instance.

I'm going to write it a couple of times so that we really solidify this concept:

Provide a product or service that people are willing to pay for.
Provide a product or service that people are willing to pay for.
Prodive a product or service that people are willing to pay for.

The natural next question is "How?" And the answer, quite simply, is to ask.

Finding your arena

There are probably a handful of Instagram accounts or small businesses or internet personalities that you like and you will gladly throw money at. Make a list of these people and businesses. Here is mine:

CONNOR'S LIST OF BUSINESSES HE LIKES

- ROOKIE mag
- VOX meDIa
- Team TReeHouse
- SCOUT BOOKS

Why do you like these businesses? What do they do well? You are a customer, and a business surrounds the need of the customer. How did these companies draw you in? Once you have identified what you like about these companies and what they do well, you have a better idea of what needs to be done with whatever business you get into. We're going to be making a lot of lists, because I love lists and lists are super helpful.

BUSINESSES you LIKE

WHY DO YOU LIKE THEM?

WHAT DO THEY DO WELL?

WHO ARE THEIR CUSTOMERS?

Of course you want to work in something that you're interested in, but the key is finding the need in the field that you're interested in. Let's say you love plants. You're probably a plant customer and buy a lot of potted plants. Your dream may be to have a shop where you sell potted plants. But here's a question you can ask yourself: Is there a need? There are tons of places that sell potted plants. You probably know all of the ones in your town. You probably go there and want to work there. You are probably not alone in this. You are their customer. The answer to the question is likely, no, there is no need for another plant shop. HOWEVER, maybe there is a need for a plant guide, because you have a lot of plants and know how to take care of them, but not a lot of other people really know. Yes there are guides to making plants already, but they're thick and ugly and not for you. Here is the need.

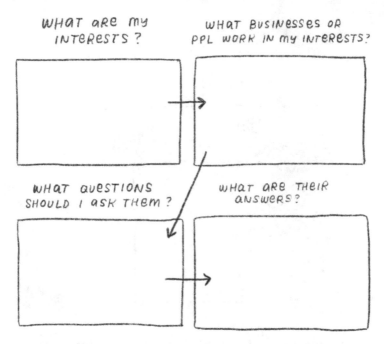

WHAT ARE MY INTERESTS?

WHAT BUSINESSES OR PPL WORK IN MY INTERESTS?

WHAT QUESTIONS SHOULD I ASK THEM?

WHAT ARE THEIR ANSWERS?

The lesson here is to start looking in the fields you are interested in, but go the extra mile and look for the gaps. If you ask the plant shop "What's the hardest part about running this plant shop?" they will likely have an answer because running a business is difficult. They will tell you their needs. You can ask your friends in the plant community "What is your least favorite thing about plant shops X, Y, and Z?" and your avid gardener friends will likely have an answer. A business provides a product or service that someone is willing to pay for. So ask. Ask a lot.

Do something

Here's a true story: I have a blog that I write on for fun. Basically I pretend that I am a staff writer for Wired Magazine. I did this as often as I could, and then one day I met a well-dressed gentleman who thought I was funny, and next thing I knew I was in a job interview for a small independent menswear boutique. He asked me if I had any writing experience (the job included writing a lot of internet content) and I was able to say "Yes, actually! I'll send you a link to my blog!"

I got the job. What was crazy was that writing on my blog sometimes felt stupid and pointless because no one really read it and it wasn't making me any money. But I did it because I liked it and provided excuses for me to pretend like I was a journalist. This silly, public side project of mine was key in finding a paying job in a cool industry. A lot of us get paralyzed and don't know how to get started. Do something. Start a Tumblr. Keep a journal. One of my favorite creators, Justin Roiland, made short animations that are incredibly stupid. They don't make sense and they have very loose plot structures but he uploaded enough of them online that he eventually got offered a spot on Adult Swim, which is how the show Rick And Morty was born. Your stupid side projects are not as stupid as you think. Finish projects and keep everything. Even if you write a really shitty, plotless TV pilot, put a bow on it just in case you meet someone cool who asks "Hey, you don't happen to know any screenwriters do you?"

These opportunities happen more often than you think. I've made incredible connections from showing people the books I've written in the past, which honestly felt ridiculous to write and often incredibly painful to finish. But, shitty or not, finish your work and have it ready to hand out. Just in case.

WHAT ARE A BUNCH OF REASONABLE
PROJECTS I CAN DO TO HAND OUT TO
INFLUENTIAL STRANGERS?

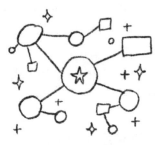

CHAPTER FIVE

NETWORKING

Oof! Networking SUCKS. People hate doing it. People are shy. People are awkward. People are anxious and self-conscious. You know what's great? Since most people feel this way, that means you are never alone in feeling like networking is the worst fucking thing on the planet. So, if you can do one small thing to make it a little less painful, DO IT. First step is realizing that networking will not kill you.

Confidence

Confidence is a finicky thing. You can fake it or you can earn it, and it is possible to do both at the same time. We perform our best when we are confident, and there are an array of ways for you to gain confidence that will help you talk to others, be self-assured, and honestly just plain-old proud of yourself.

The Victory V

There is a TED Talk on this that you should watch, but the gist is that the body and mind have such a strong connection that both have the power to influence the other. Placing yourself in power poses before a job interview dramatically increases the likelihood of you nailing the interview because you trick your body into feeling powerful and confident. The best example of a power pose is the "Victory V", which you may have seen if you ever watched someone cross the finish line of a race or nail a landing in gymnastics. You throw your hands in the air in a victorious pose, making a "V" with your triumphant arms. I do a one-minute Victory V before every single job interview, and I know that it helps me perform at my best. In any scenario that requires confidence (a date, a presentation, a debate), spending time in a Victory V will help your body feel like it is already victorious and valuable even if that isn't your natural state.

Become Batman

In Christopher Nolan's Dark Knight Trilogy, part of Batman's mythos is that he is afraid of bats and darkness, so he in turn becomes his fears in order to face them. If you are afraid of looking stupid, then I implore you to take a Batman approach and find a podium somewhere and give a 5 minute talk on something incomprehensible and very stupid. This is kind of a tall order and a hard thing for a lot of people to do. But the lessons learned are intangible: a good portion of the things we are afraid of won't kill us. We all want to be liked and loved by our peers, so often we are desperately afraid to upset them (myself included). One thing that I had a very hard time with was saying "no" to my friends, because I was afraid if I told them

I didn't want to hang out with them (because I needed to study), they wouldn't want to be my friends anymore. This was stupid and my grades suffered. In an experiment, I took a week saying "No" to everyone. Didn't matter what, but if anyone asked me for help I said "No" (this is almost definitely a Tim Ferriss trick). I became my fear and freed myself.

As far as confidence is concerned, I think a lot of us are afraid that when we introduce ourselves to new people, we are offering ourselves up for judgement and allowing for the opportunity for someone to tell us "I don't think you are worth anything." This is, of course, hyperbolic, but unfortunately it's what it feels like when we find ourselves in scenarios when we need to network or socialize. So many of my friends hate sending e-mails and making phone calls because they are afraid of saying the wrong thing. You won't die. Say the wrong thing. Apologize for saying the wrong thing. Be yourself.

Orbits

Let's think about the Sun, the Moon, and the Earth. They all travel in predictable patterns, and as a result we can predict things like the changing of the seasons, the tides, and eclipses. There is something very comforting about these patterns of movement, and it's something that I try to cultivate in my own life. Let's imagine that you are a planet.

A typical, boring, human orbit goes between home and work then back home. The duration between times you go between these things may vary slightly, but you can for the most part guarantee that at some point you will either be at home or at work. Any other stops along the way are usually cafes, restaurants, friends' houses, or the like. These are all part of your orbits. In your life, there will be some constants (home, work) and then these intermediary points between.

Now, thinking about this, you likely have a coffee shop of choice (or, if you are like me, you have a handful. Each coffee shop serves a specific purpose, usually as a fueling/resting place between gigs. I like working in cafes, and the ones that I spend the most time at are the ones that are near any of my main orbit points. Currently I am at my favorite cafe near my day job, at which I am a regular (more on this later).

Orbits are important for an assortment of reasons. In the frame of networking and relationships, it is important to realize that everyone has an orbit. Everyone has a coffee shop of choice. Everyone has haunts. Realizing this helps position yourself in circles where meeting the key individual will be much more likely.

To hammer in this concept, Cheyenne is going to draw a diagram.

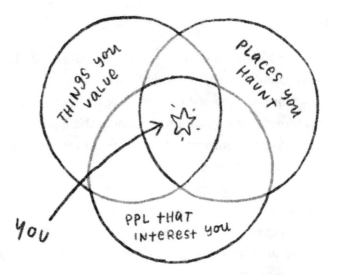

There are some places EVERYONE will go to at some point. Cafes are one of these places. Grocery stores are another. Think about how people move, think about the city you're in, and think about the kind of people you want to meet (or the kind of person you are) and what you value in the places you visit. How can you tweak your orbit for the maximum amount of gain, or the highest touch with people you want to be around?

Be a regular

Let's talk about "ambient proximity." Ambient proximity is the ability to be around someone without necessarily having to pay attention to them. I've called it "together alone time". Some people call it "studying". I don't really care what you call it. It's ambient proximity. And it depends on your orbit. And the fact of the matter is repeated ambient proximity makes you familiar, which is a good thing.

Being a familiar face at any establishment increases the likelihood that whoever is serving you will at the very least remember your name. In Portland, I was a regular at Courier Coffee. I love this place. To this day it is by far my favorite cafe in the whole world. It's a minimalist hole-in-the-wall spot across the street from Powell's City of Books, and it served as my third home. I spent so much time there that I was undoubtedly a regular, and everyone in the shop knew me and the kind of shit I was into (coffee, books). Through being a regular, I met other regulars (many of them artists, book nerds, and other people that I liked simply because they also liked this cafe) and became friends with some of the staff. At one point, I lost my apartment and was essentially homeless, and one of the baristas at Courier offered to let me live in his hallway until I got back onto my feet.

This is an atypical anecdote and I do not recommend trying to live with your baristas. But the point I am trying to illustrate is that I had a community through Courier Coffee because I was a regular. I could go on forever. The benefits of just showing up at the same spot over and over again has intangible benefits. I will probably go on just to show you how important being a regular is.

A common gripe I hear among my friends is that they have trouble meeting new people in the cities they move to. As millennials, they typically hop city to city (or neighborhood to neighborhood). They rent, they don't really have any roots tied to a specific place, so meeting people is a game that they reluctantly play and often don't play very well. Here's how to become a regular. I am going to focus on cafes because it's the easiest way to get started in this kind of thing, but feel free to apply this to sushi spots, gyms, or whatever floats your boat.

1. fiND a spot you LIke.
2. figuRe out the Best time to go to saiD spot.
3. figuRe out the optimaL FREquENCy in wHiCH you aTTeND tHis spot.
4. tweak, aDJust, aND coNTiNue to visit witH ReguLaRity.

As a general rule, going out with the intention to meet people is generally painful. Friendships, connections, any kind of networking is best formed in an organic way. Though being a regular, you become a fixture. Any kind of natural connection will happen more easily if you have a home outside your home. I am making no promises as to what you can possibly gain through being a regular somewhere, but I encourage you to experiment for a couple months to find your spot and to make it a ritual.

Strategic positioning

Pinole, California is a small town with a handful of interesting things going on in it. Don't get me wrong, I still get homesick for the place but every time I go back I know exactly why I left: there are not as many opportunities for me in Pinole as there are in Seattle, Washington (where I currently live).

This is a little bit of a no-brainer. My goals are to a) learn marketable skills b) do a shitload of interesting stuff and c) meet a lot of interesting people. If I had to choose between living in Pinole, California and Seattle, Washington, I would choose Seattle because it makes the most sense for pursuing my goals. Seattle also serves as more of springboard for new opportunities while Pinole would end up being a dead end.

Enter the concept of "strategic positioning".

There are ways for you to position yourself in the world for maximum gain. In Sun Tzu's *The Art of War* (and honestly any other text on military strategy), it is explained that in battle you should usually strive to have the higher ground. Atop a hill, you have better visibility and ultimately gravity on your side. It is WAY easier to run downhill to attack an opposing army than it is for the opposing army to run uphill. Strategic positioning.

My friend E is both a screenwriter and a tutor in Los Angeles. Through tutoring, he meets a LOT of big time producers and various celebrities and manages to develop strong connections with them which in turn brings him closer to getting a good screenwriting job. When I was a barista, I met HUNDREDS of people all the time, which was good for me living in a new city because I gained exposure to new potential friendships constantly. Networking guru Keith Ferrazzi got his start by being a golf caddy, which allowed him to spend a lot of time which affluent business people who liked to golf (which taught him a lot about how to be an affluent business person, even if he wasn't one yet).

We often hear that successful people are often in the right place at the right time. Where is the right place (and when is the right time)? Somewhere in the world, it's happening. There is a spot that is has a high density of opportunity, and it is your responsibility to find it. I mean, let's think about the Gold Rush. If you heard that people were pulling LITERAL GOLD out of the ground in California and thus securing their financial futures, you would at least CONSIDER going to this location. While I was bored out of my mind in Pinole, California, visitors from out of town would sing the praises of the Pacific Northwest, and I couldn't help but immediately pack my bags and go because it would without a doubt be a better locale for me.

I believe that instead of a dead-end, your job and your city should feel like a springboard. If you are curious, industrious, creative, and ambitious, I implore you to find a position where you feel like anything is possible. We all know what dead end feels like, and when you find a frontier, the feeling of opportunity is almost tangible in the air. This may sound a little metaphysical, and I think it is. Trusting my instincts has led me to some interesting places, and I usually could tell when a job or a location was going to be a springboard or a dead end.

WHAT ARE YOUR SPRINGBOARDS?

WHAT ARE YOUR DEAD ENDS?

DEAD END

CHAPTER SIX
CREATIVITY

Media consumption

At the time of writing this book, it is presently impossible to read every book and watch every movie/TV show in existence. I am sorry. I know. We all have The List, The Impossible List of recommendations from our friends, idols, and Twitter personalities who say that we ABSOLUTELY MUST watch X Film. Surprise: You can't do it all. Surprise: You can still have a good time.

First step is accepting that time is a finite resource. There are some things you will never watch. My go-to answer to "You have to watch this" is "No I don't." I am smart enough that I have my own list. I have a method and a system to media consumption and I am sure you have one too. And the best way to get around to consuming media is, again, to identify your goals.

WHY ARE WE WATCHING MOVIES? Or reading books? Or really doing anything? Call me old-fashioned, but watching

TV shouldn't have to feel like homework. Unless it is actually homework. For example, I watched ALL of "Breaking Bad", not because I was particularly interested in the show, but because I wanted to learn how to write good television and knew that watching "Breaking Bad" would deepen my understanding of what makes good TV. So, we're either watching for enjoyment or to further our own goals. And we don't necessarily have to take recommendations OR (more importantly) there is no real need to "keep up" with anything.

We have already established that time is a finite resource. Media, for our purposes, is infinite. Have you ever been to Powell's City of Books in Portland, Oregon? The place is filled with just about a million volumes and has three floors, nine rooms, and takes up about a city block. This is a massive bookstore. I read books pretty fast, but with balancing life, work, etc. etc., I'm reading maybe a book or two a month. Spending time reading every book I want to read wouldn't make sense. As would watching every fucking thing on Netflix. Even IF everything I read was on my List. By the time I get through my List, I will have probably already added one hundred things to my List for reading after completing my initial List.

Does this sound stupid and confusing? Good. Because it is.

TL;DR: Ride the wave.

Know your goals. Pick your media accordingly. Do not agonize over what you have missed. Grab what is within reach, and pursue what is worth pursuing.

EXAMPLE: I have heard of the movie Tampopo over and over again. I know I will love it. It is not available online. My life has been a search for a physical copy of the film so that I can finally see it because it is a WEIRD MOVIE ABOUT FOOD. Which is what I am all about. Identify what you value in the things you enjoy.

Identify the kinds of media that further you towards your goals. Navigate the sea of media with elegance. Through surfing. Taking deep dives when necessary.

What I'm trying to tell you, and I've probably already written this, is that you will not see and read everything. But instead being paralyzed by this notion, accept it and consume what you can and don't hate it. Because, I mean, it's TV.

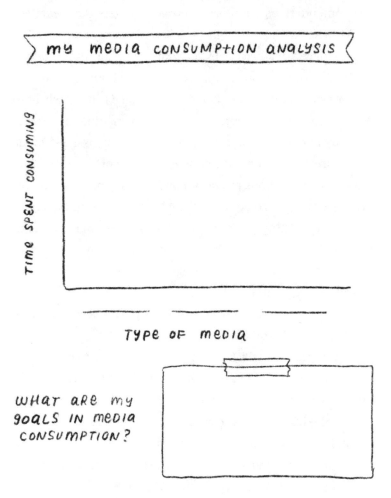

Roll the dice

Variety is the spice of life. Many a good story follows the narrative "Once upon a time [x existed]... every day [establish status quo]... UNTIL ONE DAY [status quo is ruined]". Things happen that we cannot predict. And, at least for me, this is terribly exciting. Bestselling books and movies tell me that millions of people agree. We are all interested in things that cause irreversible change. We cannot predict a vast majority of change. It is by nature random.

This is a long-winded way of saying that when crazy shit happens, it's interesting. Imagine sitting at the dinner table and say "You will NOT believe what happened today!" I can't believe it. As someone eating dinner with you, I have a rough idea of what life is typically life, and if something SO RANDOM happened that I WILL NOT BELIEVE IT, I must know.

"Life happens in the margins," my boss tells me sometimes. Some of the most beautiful things we will ever experience are spontaneous. Which means that our lives should have margins, or space for this randomness to occur.

As a generally chaotic individual, much of my life is trying to establish as much control as possible. I like predictability in my work schedule, in my finances, and in pretty much anything essential for my well-being because the recesses of my mind are chaotic and often get me into trouble. With media, I watch stuff that I like, but I also make it a point to introduce a random element into the mix. I often allocate about ten percent of my media consumption to be focused on the things that I would never normally consume.

Randomness is important. In computer programming, in order create anything seemingly natural or organic, programmers use functions that generate random numbers to color in what carefully outlined processes cannot. Thus, if you want anything to be life-like, you need a random element to it.

Rolling dice, picking up a random book, letting the internet tell you what songs to listen to, all are ways to get out of your normal habits, tastes, and rhythms. Ten percent seems like a reasonable amount of random by my estimates, but I encourage you to experiment with more or less as you see fit.

Keep everything

It sucks to miss an opportunity. It's an incredible feeling to nab one. One of the most important things is to have a goal (as we discussed earlier) so that you can prepare when that Big Moment comes. You know the one I'm talking about. There will be a moment when the Key Person meets you at a dinner party and they say, "Hey, I'm looking for someone who [does exactly what you do]," and in this moment you should have something to slide across the table. What do you slide across the table? Is it a business card? Does the business card have a website? What's on the website? Can you show this Key Person a place where all of your Incredible Work is located?

For this reason, KEEP EVERYTHING. It is super hard to make a portfolio without anything to fill it with. Beginnings, half-finished projects, stubs, I don't care. Whatever you have, hold onto it. A pile of trash can turn into a neatly organized booklet that demonstrates your potential. I'll emphasize that finishing stuff and having polished projects is a good idea, but I am often surprised at how impressed people are by the things that I kind of, well, shat out. In one of my document tubs, I have all my little notebooks with my stupid little poems in them, and when I read excerpts to my friends they fucking love it. Sometimes they even work at open mics. I'm glad I have them.

It is also a point of confidence to look at the pile of shit you do and think "Damn I'm really something aren't I?" I know sometimes I get super frustrated and want to throw away everything I've ever done and to start from scratch. I'm glad I didn't, especially when I am trying to prove to others that I make stuff.

Furthermore, keeping everything helps one identify patterns. You may notice, in reviewing all of your projects, things that work and things that didn't. You may notice trends or recurring subjects that you hadn't noticed before. This is incredibly valuable information. Keep it. Use it. Ascend.

CHAPTER SEVEN

HOME LIFE & SELF-CARE

You need to eat, sleep, and drink water

I find it ridiculous that so many of us (myself included) forget or ignore the fact that we are human beings that at the end of the day need to do a handful of things: eat, sleep, and drink water. We work so that we can eat, sleep, and drink water. Because at the end of the day, we can't be creative, we can't send love into the world, and we can't ride Space Mountain if we do not eat, sleep, or drink water.

It sometimes help me center myself to take a step back and examine these core life processes. If I feel like garbage, I'll take a moment to plot out how to make sure I will get the proper amount of food, rest, and water. If you cover these main and essential needs and have them down pat, you are going to be that much better positioned to kick ass in your professional and creative life. One of the reasons human beings became so fucking smart is because they figured out how to start farming, which allowed them to stop worrying about whether or not they would have food the next day. Taking care of the basics frees up the mind for higher thought. Do not (I repeat, DO NOT) avoid eating, sleeping, and hydration. It's easy to forget, but incredibly destructive to not honor these needs.

Here's what I do: I don't fuck around with my core habits of eating, sleeping, and drinking water. I'll share with you my schedule, but this time we're going to look at it through the lens of staying alive and healthy.

⩫ THE RECIPE ⩪

6:30 am	WAKE UP
7:00 am	COFFEE
8:00 am	BREAKFAST
12:30 pm	LUNCH
3:00 pm	COFFEE
7:00 pm	DINNER
11:00 pm	SLEEP

So, this is the framework. What's cool about frameworks is that you don't always have to stick to them, but you can always fall back on them. I do all of this without thinking. It seems like it should be pretty easy to do, but I know, I *know* it's hard. Try it out. Once your body settles into a rhythm, it's unstoppable. Make this habit, for the love of yourself and all that you do.

WHaT DOeS YOUR DaILY FRAMEWORK LOOK LIKE?

Time	ACTIVITY

You need to relax

I just got back from a vacation. It was incredible. I made a focused effort to unwind and not to work. Fortunately, Cheyenne was with me and was able to keep me in check. We made sure that neither of us worked, and instead spent our time lounging about and enjoying sights, sounds, and sunshine.

The funny thing about relaxing is that it is productive. This sounds crazy but it's not. If you are trying to be productive all the time and never relax, you are going to get stuck in modes of thinking that are counter-productive. By staring at your computer screen and wondering what you should be doing, you are beating yourself up instead of taking care of yourself. Naps, breaks, and walks all refresh the brain and increase your potential for output. On my vacation, I was astounded at the ideas and plans my brain came up with when I wasn't actively trying to ideate.

Mini-vacations exist. Don't beat yourself up about it. Be honest about when you are procrastinating and when you are taking a much needed break. If you journal (or simply pay attention) you can identify the right time to rest. I know for me, I can feel the "wall", or the moment when I'm just staring at my screen and not doing anything. This is when I walk away and go outside or change location. I am then refreshed. Sometimes that's all it takes. Whether your vacation is a week or an afternoon, give yourself one when you need it. Don't ignore your body when it is tired.

You need to have a good time

One of my best friends is Z. He might be the smartest person I know. He works very hard, is always three steps ahead of the curve, and always has a business idea. One day, he came to me with an epiphany.

"Today, I thought about the things that really make me happy," he said. "I wrote a list. Basically, it's snacking, playing video games, and watching dope ass movies. And after writing this list, I realized how long it had been since I had done any of these things. That's crazy. I love this stuff but I totally forgot that it existed."

Again, a by-product of finding flow: you forget basic shit, like snackin' and playing video games. The happy ending to this story is that Z spent the following weekend playing video games with friends. We need to remind ourselves that we are allowed to have fun. Not everything we do has to be productive or valuable. Personally, one of the things that I love doing is listening to hip hop. It's a simple joy and has no end goal other than to enjoy myself. When I cook food, I sometimes see it as an excuse to listen to hip hop. I see walking/commuting the same way. It is just 100% a pleasurable experience.

As freelance-y folk, we have a tendency to try and turn everything, especially the things we enjoy, into monetizable ventures. It is SO important to have things that you do for fun's sake. It's good for the soul and amplifies the magic of doing something because you like it, not because it's valuable. This sounds like a good time to make a list! What are the things that you like to do for fun's sake? I'll write one too.

WHaT DO you DO FOR fuN?

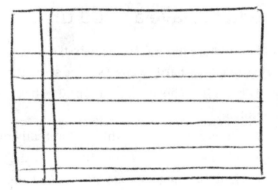

CONNOR'S LISt:

- HIP HOP!
- comic BOOKS!
- RICK & MORTY!
- BOJaCK HORSEMAN!
- BaNaNagRaMS!
- BOggLe!
- OTHeR BOaRD games!
- FRISBee!
- MaKINg PLayLISTS!
- SHOOTIN' the SHIT w/ FRIeNDS!
- FaNCy ResTaURaNTS WITH CHey!

I think it's good to make sure you distinguish clear lines between your fun stuff and your profitable passion. This way, your fun stuff will always be there when you're sad, and it will never feel like work. As an A-type, I love to work, but I know maybe I love it a little too much. The problem here is not beating yourself up. All of the advice in this chapter is mainly geared towards loving yourself, and this particular step is probably the most literal and straightforward way of going about it.

You need to manage your money

Being an adult, as we have noticed, is being smart about how you manage your resources. One of these resources is money. Money allows us to function in a community of people exchanging goods and services. Yes, the love of money can lead to corruption and greed, but if you instead think of it as a tool rather than an end goal, you are already better off. The reason I bring up this distinction is that money gets a bad rap. People with tons of money aren't very popular among those who have none, and people sometimes will trade the things they care about in the pursuit of financial security. This is a grandiose problem that I won't be able to solve in this book. But what I can do is help you reframe how you think about money.

Be Real

Kid Ink has a song titled "Be Real" that I encourage you to listen to 1) because it's a bop and 2) it's an easy way to remember how to start getting your money situation together. Be honest. When budgeting, don't focus on how you'd like to spend your money or plotting out your grocery habits in the way that you'd like to be. First, I want you to take a look at how you are spending your money. It will be hard to look at. I know when I first started budgeting, I was shocked and ashamed at how much money I spent at bars. Even this year, I looked at my bank statements and realized I was spending more on restaurants than I was spending on rent. Ouch.

This will hurt at first, but one you accept the truth of where your money is going, you can start to make changes. I used Mint (an online app you may have heard of) to get reports back on what I spend most of my money on. The app isn't perfect, but it showed me enough that I knew the major ways I could save money included cutting back on restaurants and coffee. By making myself lunch and brewing coffee at home, I save $500 a month. $500! That's crazy, and I would never have been able to make this change if I shied away from scrutinizing my bank account.

Whether you use Mint, your bank statement, or saved receipts, go through each month and add up repeat expenses. Knowledge is half the battle. Next, I want you to think about values. Again.

Values. Again.

As we have established near the beginning of the book, getting your values together gives you focus. With finances, knowing what you value means you can prioritize how you spend your money to maximize your value. As Ramit Sethi states in his book I Will Teach You To Be Rich, most people don't really want to be rich, they just want to feel rich. And feeling rich means spending money on things you like.

I value my time in coffee shops more than I value the convenience of buying lunch on my break. So, I bring a bag lunch to allow me more resources to spend at cafes. I value my ability to interact with my community more than I value world travel (for now), so I take less trips out of the country and instead take a Lyft from places to place to meet up with my various social circles. For you, you may love fancy dinners. Or watches. Or quality time with friends. Once you identify the things you want to spend time and money on, you are able to more responsibly allocate what little means you have for a life that works for you.

Getting Paid

Making more money is helpful. It is hard, but if it was easy, everyone would be doing it. If you want to get paid more, you have to work to figure out how to make this happen. It often means challenging your assumptions, doing something you are unfamiliar with, or sustaining daily study and practice. Know this: people who work super hard to make more money are not happier than you are. Yes, they don't have the same problems you have, but money can never, ever substitute happiness. I believe that once you make enough money to get your baseline needs covered, happiness depends solely on you and whether or not you are living in line with your values. It's a tricky, ethereal thing, happiness, but it is important to know that as you grind at your hustle, you can be happy now. Money is a point system. It's a game we play, and it is up to you to play the game well.

CONCLUSION

When I first tried writing the conclusion to this book, my computer crapped out. I was in a cafe with Cheyenne and we were all set to work, when all of the sudden - nothing. We've all been there, but it felt particularly annoying because I was trying to write a book about getting it together, but there are seemingly always setbacks that come out of nowhere.

You can't plan for everything. Even if you draw up business plans, wake up on time, and budget properly, something unexpected is bound to happen and make your journey seem impossible. It's times like these when I think about my friend J. J is the chillest dude I know. I once watched him realize that his identity was stolen as he browsed through his bank account on his phone. He chuckled, called the bank, and got it taken care of. "You are the calmest person I've ever spoken to when their identity has been stolen," said the person on the other end of the line. "Haha no doubt," replied J.

Furthermore, one late night Cheyenne locked herself out of her car, and it seemed like it was going to be the end of the world. Fortunately, J and I were both around to help out, but J knew exactly who to call, how much the services would cost, and how to keep everyone calm and chipper. It took waiting until three in the morning, but AAA came and fixed the situation, and everything turned out fine.

The lesson here is that we get to choose how we react to certain situations. We can't plan for everything, but we can orient our minds so that when the unexpected happens, we are unfazed. Instead of giving up, we find solutions, and instead of hiding from our problems, we learn. When my laptop crapped out, I was upset. But I opened up my notebook and started a rough draft of this conclusion. We all have to make do with the cards we are dealt.

And it's this system of being adaptable, especially in unpredictable terrain, because the real sustainable loop, the one that will help us the most, is our ability to fail, learn, and to try again. Life is one big experiment of comparing advice to our realities. There's a quote that my theatre professor in college used to read to us, and I find it appropriate here: "I am hurt but I am not slain, / I'll lay me down and bleed a while, / then I'll rise and fight again." This is from an old English folk song that you can look up on Google, but the point is that you are allowed to have a bad day. Honor your setbacks, rest, and then get back out there.

hi! this is cheyenne! you're
amazing and you totally got this!!

Hello! This is Connor.
I agree with Chey.

we got ur back xx
(stay bRILLIANt!)

CPSIA information can be obtained
at www.ICGtesting.com
Printed in the USA
BVHW030228110121
597531BV00011B/443